MW01155693

Dedicated to Thor who opened up a whole new world to me and showed his love so completely, my husband Brad who supported me through this entire journey, Sydney O. Schultz who encouraged me, and to the hundreds of Thor the Deer friends on Facebook who found love and inspiration in this story.

One day in May, a *teeny* *baby* deer was born.

Little Thor woke up in a pile of leaves
on the soft ground under a warm, bright sun.

All around him,
he heard birds chirping
cheep cheep!
bugs buzzing
bzzzzzzz!
and wind in the trees
whoosh!

But what he didn't hear was his **mama**.
She was completely **gone**.

Alone, Thor **waited** and **waited**,
but she never reappeared.

"Eeeeee! Eeeeee!"

he cried as he became
very, very **hungry.**

Finally, Thor got to his feet
and began to wander, slowly
walking out onto a lawn.

"Eeeeee! Eeeeee!"

he cried again to anyone
who could hear.

At that moment, Brad
was working in the yard
and heard the fawn.

He looked over
and saw

tiny Thor,
who came over to
stand by his feet.

Stepping gently away,
Brad then went up to the
house and told his wife, Dawn,
**"Come quick!
A baby deer is
on the lawn!"**

Dawn's heart melted
when she saw Thor alone
in the grass and realized
he needed **help.**

He was such a tiny thing,
she thought.

**Where in the world
was his momma?**

Dawn stepped closer
to take a better look.

But Thor became **scared**
and crept back into the
poison oak to hide.

Dawn then knew they needed to **help** the little fawn. She called the vet, who said to bring tiny Thor in for a check-up.

Dawn had to step into the poison oak but didn't care. She knew Thor needed to see the doctor, so she gently lifted him out and held him in her arms.

Dawn and Brad then bundled Thor in a **cozy** blanket and drove him to the vet.

Good news!
Thor was healthy but now needed a mom.

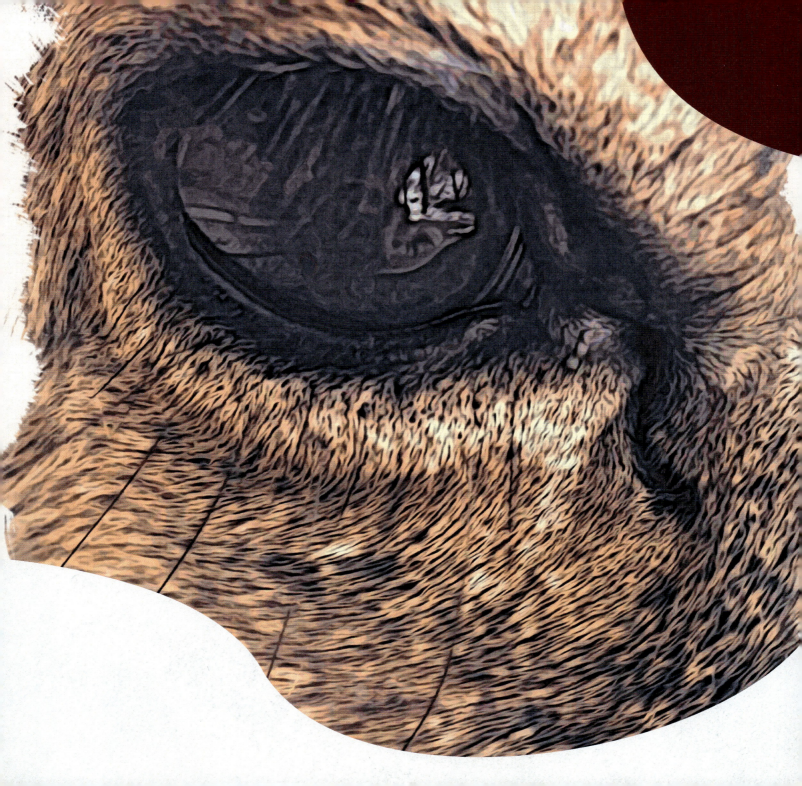

Surprised, Dawn and Brad looked at each other, suddenly realizing they were new parents to a 6-pound fawn!

They both looked at Thor, who blinked back at them with his soft, brown eyes.

Who could not love such a cute little deer?

They headed back home with Thor, where he spent the first week sleeping on blankets inside the house since he needed milk every few hours.

Being indoors also **protected** Thor from scary animals like coyotes, which would love to eat a baby deer as a snack!

Every few hours throughout the night, Dawn got up and heated milk up to feed Thor. Baby deer are hungry, just like human babies!

When drinking warm milk, his happy squeaks made Dawn's heart grow full of love for this tiny creature.

"MMMmmmm, Eeeee!"

Thor said as he guzzled his milk, his bright brown eyes shining.

OH NO!
Here came Harley
and Tabitha!

The two cats came by to say "hi" and touched Thor's nose. Curious about these new creatures, he moved toward them but froze as their eyes got big and their tails rose.

"MEOWWWW!"

said the cats to each other, but soon they realized that Thor wouldn't hurt them. Satisfied, they walked away with a flick of their whiskers.

After a week, Thor was ready to leave the house; it was time to move him **outside.**

Brad built a pen outside for Thor to sleep at night, safe from the animals creeping around in the night. With bushes and trees, it was a **comfy hiding place.**

Dawn, still worried about keeping Thor safe, set up a tent inside the pen.

She slept there for almost two months so she could get up to feed Little Thor his milk in the middle of the night while holding a flashlight.

When Cody Coyote came around to sniff and howl, Dawn was listening and crawled out of the tent to scare him off, making a great big

"YOWLLL!!!"

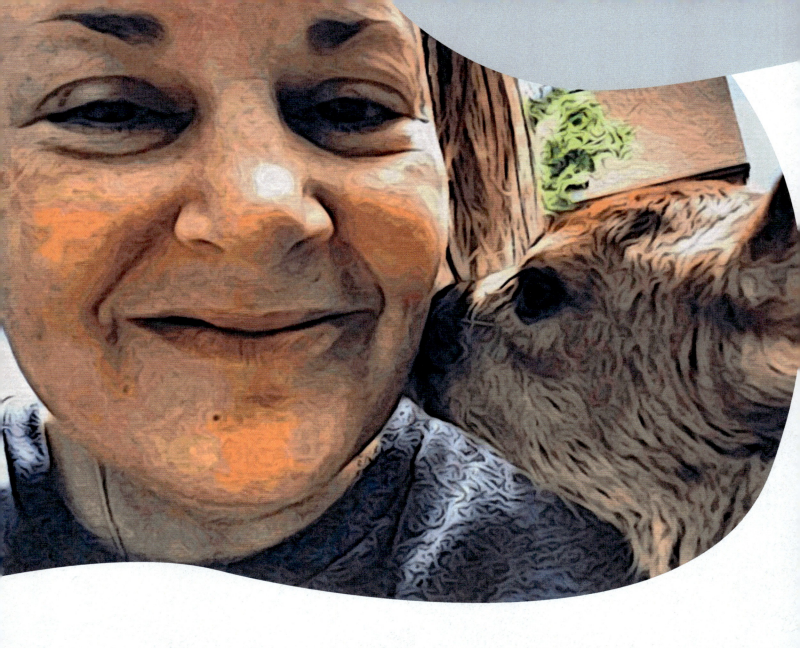

After each meal, she cuddled Thor, and in return,
he licked her and tried to nibble her ear.

His warm breath and quiet **"squee"** next to her face became something Dawn loved to hear, knowing that Thor loved her as much she loved him.

As he ate more and more, Thor's legs grew longer, and he learned how to run, including how to play chase. Dawn ran, and then Thor ran too.

How many times do you see a deer and person playing together?

They both had
so much fun!

Being a mom to a deer was new to Dawn, and sometimes, she wasn't sure quite what to do. But she watched, guessed, and then **did her best.**

Thor continued to **grow,** and he explored the woods more and more as spring turned into summer.

His fur picked up all sorts of scratchy things like burrs, ticks, and fleas.

Thor would come up to the house and look at Dawn to let her know that it was time for **brushing.**

Picking up the brush, she would feel with her fingers then comb all of these icky things out while Thor stood there, patiently waiting.

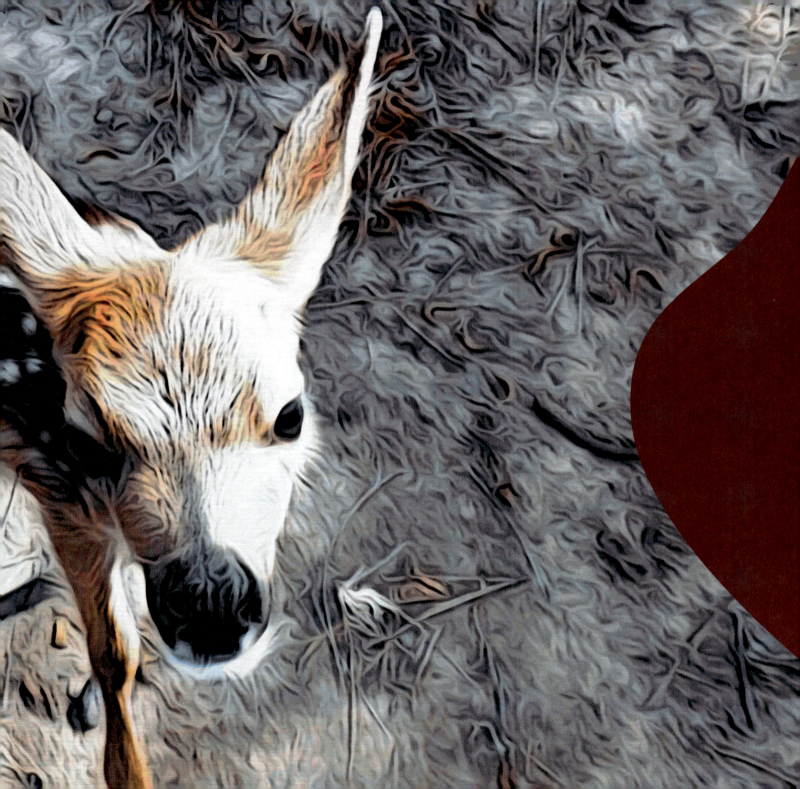

His **coat** was tan with white spots from head to tail, and it was incredibly soft.

There was no smell because fawns are born that way so predators can't find them.

Thor's fur was silkiest under his chin, and when Dawn brushed it, she was sure she saw him **grin** in happiness.

Their connection became a bond so strong it would never break. Because they spent so much time together, Thor was **always** right there any time Dawn went outside.

"THOR!" Dawn would call outside in the morning, letting him know that his warm milk was ready.

clump! clump! clump!

At the sound of her voice, Thor would leap onto the deck and land with a thud. His tail fluffed out and went straight up, and his giant ears bent forward.

It was now time for food, and boy was he was hungry! **YUMMM**

As summer turned into fall, the time finally came that little Thor had to learn to eat other **yummy** things, including apples, plums, berries, and leaves.

Dawn started showing him the kinds of foods she had seen the other deer nibbling.

Walking around the woods, Thor began to eat what adult deer eat, and his favorite foods became acorns, grass, leaves, and lichen.

There was so much food everywhere he looked!

And as Thor got older, it was time to meet his real family. The other deer that visited often were his aunts, uncles, and cousins.

Did you know that deer can tell family members by smell?

All the fawns began
dashing through the
trees to dart and to play.
Thor ran and jumped,
starting to realize that
he was a deer.

He began looking
forward to the other
fawns being around
as **new friends and
playmates.**

Dawn smiled. Her heart loved Thor so much, but she knew that this little deer needed to be **free and wild** with his deer family. Dawn knew it was wrong to try to keep him as a pet.

Being in the wild also meant Thor had to learn what to like and what to fear.

It sounded like Cody Coyote was near, and Thor's tiny hooves got ready to fly!

Did you know that deer have cool grooves on their hooves?

They walk on their tiptoes —
can you?

Thor's long, warm ears constantly swiveled and twitched, testing every sound and letting him know what was around and if he needed to get ready to run from Cody Coyote.

No, not this time.
It was just another deer.

Then, one day, there were some new arrivals. Wild turkeys came wandering in while Thor ate clover under the clear blue sky.

"gobble gobble!"

said Tom Turkey, and his head began to wobble.

He turned and looked at Thor, then looked again. Tom Turkey couldn't believe what he saw: A deer and a human were side by side!

Animals and people indeed can share a bond, but that also means that each needs to **respect** each other's place in the world.

Those bonds of friendship and trust were still there because Thor and Dawn loved each other.

However, they both knew that Thor couldn't turn Dawn into a deer any more than Dawn could make Thor into a person.

In August, Thor, Dawn, and Brad were outside when they all smelled **smoke.** First, just a faint whiff, then stronger. The sky got dark, and burnt leaves started falling on the house.

Dawn's phone rang; the police told everyone to leave because a fast-moving **fire** was nearby.

Brad and Dawn both started running around the house, loading up their essential things. Thor stood outside, scared because of the smoke but not sure what to do.

Dawn loaded up the car then went over to Thor, who looked up into her eyes.

She nodded, then opened up the car door, and he jumped right in.

He was part of the family, too!

The little deer enjoyed the ride, looking at lots of new things.

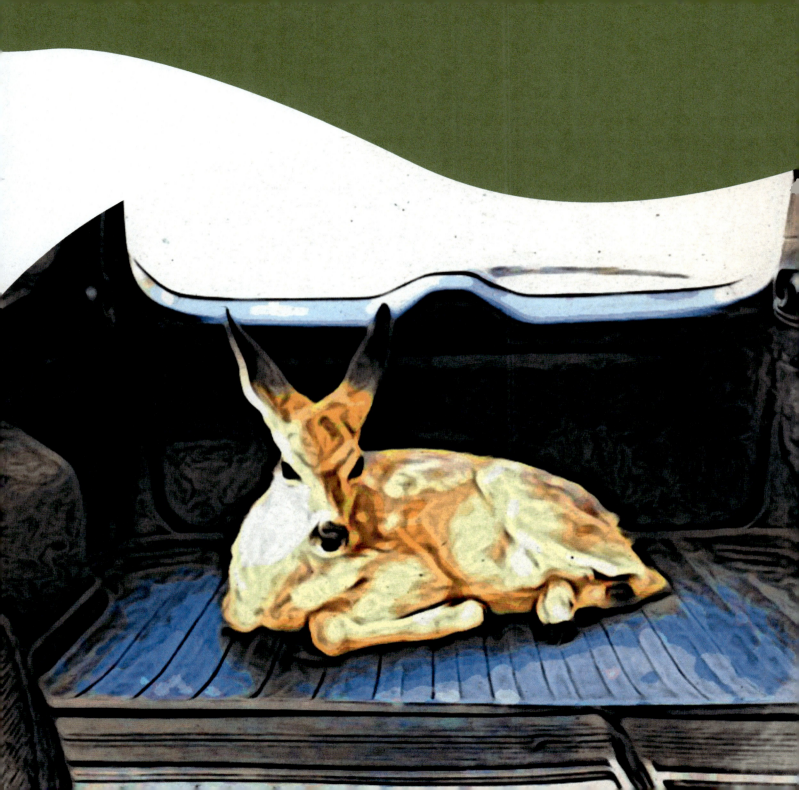

Can you imagine the sight of a deer sticking its head out of a car while sitting in the front seat?

Neither can other people, but they saw Thor as Dawn drove down the road, and **wow,** they were surprised!

The firefighters put the fire out quickly, and everyone got to return home. Thor was very excited to hop out of the car and be back home.

He shook his head and
stamped his feet, then quickly
ran up the hill into the trees
to take a long nap.

Soon, the seasons started to change. The days flew by, and Thor soon became a **fine young buck.**

He started to spend more time in the woods away from the house, and his little antler buttons began popping up.

Dawn knew their days together were nearly over. She and Brad took Thor for longer walks to show him more of his **territory.**

Did you know that deer stay within one square mile, which is their home range?

Dawn treasured every moment with Thor. She loved how he would come running to catch up with her in the woods and give her hand a lick as if to say, **"I love you!"**

"Will we always be friends?" she wondered.

Throughout the winter, Dawn saw Thor off and on, his visits less often. Yearling bucks spend time together, leaving their mommas behind because they are now grown up.

**Then one day
in the spring,**
Thor stretched his legs
and stood tall, ready join
his deer cousins.

With a nod to Dawn, a nudge, and a lick, he bounded away.

Dawn watched with tears in her eyes, sad to see her friend disappear but happy that she had helped raise a beautiful buck into becoming the best deer he could be.

The End

DID YOU KNOW?

BLACK-TAILED DEER FUN FACTS:

 Deer have 4 toes on each foot – two hooves in front, and two smaller ones higher up on the back side of their leg.

The average lifespan of a deer is 6-7 years for males, and up to 12 years for females.

Black-tailed deer have very fuzzy ears which helps filter out the wind so they can hear things better.

Fawns nurse from their mothers for about 4-5 months before they are weaned.

The only touching between deer that happens regularly is between doe and fawn. They groom each other and creates a strong bond.

Mama deer get pregnant in the fall and give birth usually in April / May.

 Fawns do not have any scent in the first months of their lives; later, they smell like dry leaves and grass.

Grown-up bucks can weigh up to 200 pounds
and stand about 3 ½ feet high at the shoulder.

Antlers on bucks get the biggest around 4-5 years of age. Each year, the
buck sheds its antlers, then new ones start growing in, covered in velvet
which gives the antlers lots of blood to help them get bigger.

Deer have four stomachs and chew their
cud as part of their eating process.

The favorite food of deer includes acorns, grass, lichen,
fruit, nuts, and the tender leaves on bushes. They will
also eat leaves on trees.

Deer make sounds... the fawns make a kind of "EEEEE!" and the mothers
call out in more of a groan. The bucks roar during the rut when they are
fighting with their antlers.

Deer are one of the few animals that can eat
poison oak – and it doesn't make them itchy!

Deer have their own customs when near other herd members; looking
directly at each other is considered aggressive and can cause
problems, so deer mostly glance over quickly to others without staring.

If you find what you think is an abandoned baby or injured animal, contact your local wildlife rehabilitation center for assistance. Many babies are left alone while mothers are off finding food, so disturbing them actually hurts their chances for survival. Contacting authorities will ensure that the animal is handled appropriately.